ANNIE SLOAN

DECORATIVE
WOOD FINISHES

A PRACTICAL GUIDE

ANNIE SLOAN

DECORATIVE
Wood FINISHES

A PRACTICAL GUIDE

Photography by Geoff Dann

THE READER'S DIGEST ASSOCIATION, INC.
Pleasantville, New York/Montreal

A Reader's Digest Book

Conceived, edited, and designed by
Collins & Brown Limited

Editor Colin Ziegler
Assistant Editor Claire Waite
Art Director Roger Bristow
Designer Steve Wooster
DTP Designer Claire Graham
Photographer Geoff Dann

The acknowledgments that appear on page 96 are hereby made a
part of this copyright page.

Library of Congress Cataloging in Publication Data:

Sloan, Annie. 1949–
    Decorative wood finishes : a practical guide / Annie Sloan ;
photography by Geoff Dann.
      p. cm.
    Includes index.
    ISBN 0-89577-928-5
    1. Furniture finishing. 2. Finishes and finishing.   I. Title.
TT199.4.S56   1997
684. 1' 043–dc21   96-37367

Printed in Portugal

Contents

Introduction

Painting and Embellishing Wood

BELOW The fine tradition of embellishing wood using hand painting (see pp. 28–33), stenciling, and metal leaf is very old. Here, a stencil was used to create the main part of the design. This was made to look more individual with hand-painted lines and dots.

D ECORATIVE WOOD FINISHES is about decorating woods using paints, stains, waxes, and varnishes without losing the interest and beauty of the wood's natural grain. There is such a magnificent variety of woods available, each exhibiting different types of grain – some smooth and narrow, others coarse and wide, some knotted and others curled – and while you may generally think of wood as brown in color, closer inspection reveals that it can be almost white, gray, almost black, or deep red, or have a pink tinge. Some woods, like sandalwood and cedar, are even scented.

All of these woods can be enhanced and embellished using the techniques illustrated in this book. Traditional wood finishing materials are used like wax and pigment stains and the abundant range of modern products now available such as precolored stains and varnishes.

Woodgraining

ABOVE In the past, pine, which is so popular today, was considered too plain to display in its natural state. Instead, it was painted to look like a more elaborate wood using special combs and brushes (see pp. 34–39). This pine door was woodgrained using two different wood effects, bird's eye maple in the center and oak grain on the stiles and rails.

In the past, particularly during the 18th century, painting designs on wood and embellishing the surface with metal leaf was very popular (see pp. 28–33). The finer, more decorative woods, such as satinwood, were not completely covered with paint, rather flowers and classical motifs were added so that these painted decorations complimented the wood surface. The technique of *Revealing Wood Under Paint*, where paint is removed from a wood surface in patterns (see pp. 40–43), is a natural extension of this tradition of painted furniture. The contrast of opaque paint and a strong grain of the wood is very attractive. Anyone who has stripped a piece of paint-covered furniture may have toyed with pattern-making with the paint stripper to reveal the grain underneath. You can also use paint on wood to give plain pieces of furniture an aged look by distressing the painted surface (see pp. 44–47). Or use combs and graining rollers over a mixture of glaze and paint to imitate the grain of woods such as oak and bird's eye maple with the *Woodgraining* technique (see pp. 34–39).

Painting and Distressing

BELOW The charm of old painted pieces of furniture lies in the way that the paint wears away over the years to reveal glimpses of the wood underneath. You can recreate this effect using wax and water-base paints over crackleglaze medium (see pp. 44–47).

Revealing Wood Under Paint

ABOVE You can use paint stripper or masking fluid as here to strip away parts of a solidly painted surface to reveal the wood beneath (see pp. 40–43). The contrast of plain, flat paint and decorative wood gives this technique its particular appeal.

Using stains, both homemade and modern proprietary varieties (see pp. 52–55 and 56–61), is a simple way to transform a piece of wood. Stains can create a period look, if you use brown tones and black, or can look very modern if you use bright primary colors, sometimes overlaid so that glimpses of the first color are obvious.

Penwork (see pp. 68–71), in which you use dark-colored inks to create an opaque layer of decoration over wood, was a traditional 18th-century technique, used particularly over fine but plainly grained wood. And from the restorer's workshop we learn the techniques of *Fuming and Bleaching* (see pp. 62–67). Using these techniques, in conjunction with incising, some masking tape and masking fluid, you can transform simple pieces into modern masterpieces.

The simplest way to bring out the beauty of the wood is to either wax or varnish it. A white wax, for instance, is a dramatic way of drawing attention to the grain of dark oak. You can gain added interest by coloring waxes and varnishes with pigments (see pp. 76–79 and 80–85) and using them to stencil or create your own patterns.

Using Homemade Stains

ABOVE *Homemade stains (see pp. 52–55) are simply made using basic materials such as pigments, Van Dyck crystals, and ferrous sulfate mixed with water. This lampbase was partially stained using Van Dyck crystals, creating a dark brown stain.*

Using Modern Stains

ABOVE *Modern stains (see pp. 56–61) come in premixed form so you can use them straight from the can. For pale, soft, or bright colors on softwoods you use water-base products. This tabletop was incised with a sharp knife and then stained with deep, strong, oil-base stains, which are more suitable for hardwoods.*

Fuming and Bleaching

ABOVE *You can darken wood using the fumes from ammonia carbonate to give a piece an aged look, or lighten wood using a speciality two-part wood bleach. Fuming and bleaching (see pp. 62–67) are techniques used by the restorer but you can also use them in a decorative way. This block of wood shows its normal color in the middle with fumed and bleached corners above and below.*

Finally, you can combine some of the techniques in this book to create a stunning and individual effect (see pp. 86–91).

Throughout the book you will find step-by-step instructions, and color combinations to try, potential pitfalls to avoid, and countless ideas showing you how to use the techniques on large and small pieces of furniture. The information on preparing your surface, choosing a technique to suit your wood surface, and finishing and protecting your work will ensure you get the best results.

Experiment with the different techniques in *Decorative Wood Finishes* and you will learn how to enhance the inherent beauty of wood in the most appealing way. You will also find that the possibilities for decorating and embellishing wood are almost infinite.

Penwork

ABOVE You can contrast finely grained woods with a decoration in ink using the traditional technique of penwork (see pp. 68–71). You usually use India ink, which is black, or sepia drawing ink, but you can also use ordinary writing ink for a more transparent effect. The penwork on this panel was done in India ink inspired by an antique marquetry design.

Using Colored Waxes

ABOVE You can use the mellow softness of waxes (see pp. 76–79) in a decorative way rather than simply as a finish. Add pigments to clear or neutral wax to give furniture an overall color or use them when stenciling. Here, white wax was rubbed into the grain of the chair legs to emphasize their markings.

Using Colored Varnishes

ABOVE Generally, varnish is used as a finish for wood, but in this technique (see pp. 80–85) it is also used decoratively. Add pigments or bronze powder to clear varnish or use a proprietary precolored varnish. This gives furniture an overall translucent color or can be used to make patterns, like the stripes on these blocks of wood.

Preparing Surfaces

To ENSURE SUCCESSFUL results, a wooden surface should be smooth and free of imperfections before it is decorated. To remove old coats of wax, dirt, paint, or varnish and to seal and smooth out your wooden surface (see pp. 12–14), use the tools and materials on this page. When preparing surfaces wear a pair of sturdy protective gloves that protect the hands from chemicals and allow you to really attack a piece of furniture with steelwool and scrapers.

Cotton Cloth

RIGHT A supply of cotton cloth is essential when preparing furniture. It is used to wipe brushes, clean surfaces, and to mop up spills.

Cotton cloth

Tools for Stripping Paint and Varnish

BELOW You can use any kind of bristle brush to apply paint stripper to your surface. When stripping a carved piece, a small bristle brush is ideal for reaching into the crevices. Always wear protective gloves when using paint stripper. Use coarse steelwool to remove paint or varnish after the application of paint stripper.

Coarse steelwool

Scrapers

BELOW There are many scrapers you can use to remove paint or varnish which is already softened by paint stripper or to smooth out an uneven wooden surface.

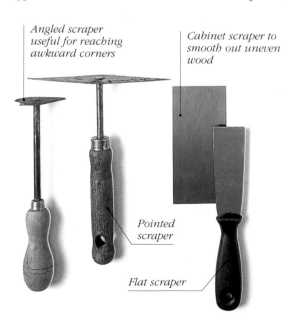

Angled scraper useful for reaching awkward corners

Cabinet scraper to smooth out uneven wood

Pointed scraper

Flat scraper

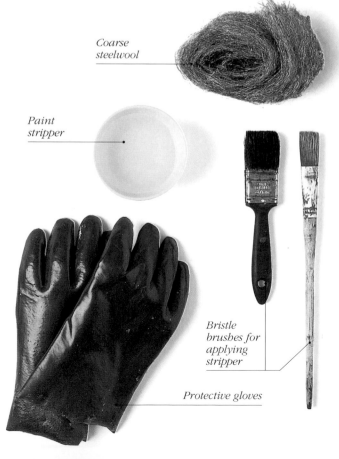

Paint stripper

Bristle brushes for applying stripper

Protective gloves

Tools for Cleaning Furniture

RIGHT AND BELOW An old piece which is dirty or has a wax finish but has a good patina can be cleaned and revived with a proprietary furniture cleaner only.

Proprietary furniture cleaner

Cotton cloth for wiping off excess cleaner

Soft steelwool for applying cleaner

Bleach

BELOW Some pieces of furniture are marked with water marks, ring marks, and ink stains. To remove these use a one-part wood bleach (see p. 14), also known as oxalic acid.

Proprietary one-part wood bleach and vegetable-fiber brush for applying it

Face mask to be worn while using bleach

Neutralizer specified in manufacturer's instructions

Fuller's Earth

RIGHT Fuller's earth, available from hardware stores or speciality suppliers, is a very fine powder which is used to remove very bad oil marks from furniture.

Fuller's earth

Tack Cloth

RIGHT Tack cloth, available at hardware stores or from speciality suppliers, is a cloth with a waxy feel that picks up fine dust after sanding.

Tack cloth

Tools for Sealing Wood

RIGHT Sanding sealer is a denatured alcohol/methylated spirit based liquid used to seal the wood surface so that paint or stain is not absorbed into the wood. It is available from hardware stores or speciality suppliers. Sandpaper takes off the shiny surface of the sealer (see p. 12) and smooths the surface of any wood.

Sandpaper of various grades

Fine steelwool for finishing sanding sealer

Sanding sealer and brush for applying it

The amount of preparation needed on any piece of furniture depends on its age. Newly cut wood should not need cleaning but if the technique you plan to use relies on the product being absorbed into the wood – for example, *Using Homemade Stains* (see pp. 52–55) and *Using Modern Stains* (see pp. 56–61) – you may want to raise the grain (see below) to improve the absorbency of the wood. For other techniques, including *Painting and Embellishing Wood* (see pp. 28–33), *Woodgraining* (see pp. 34–39), and *Penwork* (see pp. 68–71) you need to seal the wood, making it less absorbent, using sanding sealer (see p. 11).

Raising the Grain

1 After sanding the surface with coarse sandpaper, use a clean cloth soaked in water to dampen the surface. The water swells the wood and raises the grain.

2 When the surface is dry, rub the wood to a smooth surface using medium-grade sandpaper. Wrap the sandpaper around a cork block if you find this easier.

Using Sanding Sealer

1 Apply the sanding sealer with a paintbrush. The sealer is colorless and it is easy to miss areas, so work systematically. Allow to dry according to the manufacturer's instructions.

2 In the direction of the grain, lightly rub the sealed surface with medium-grade sandpaper. This takes away the shine of the sealer and reveals any missed areas.

3 If necessary, apply a second coat of sealer (inset) and let dry. Rub down the surface with fine steelwool to remove any excess sealer that has not been absorbed.

When decorating secondhand furniture, floors, or doors it will be difficult to ascertain what products have been used on them in the past, but you will probably need to remove coats of paint or varnish and clean away old wax, dirt, and stubborn stains to obtain a smooth surface. Old veneers may have cracks, which are easily repaired using a hard, sealing wax available in stick form from hardware and speciality stores (see p. 15). When doing any of the techniques on these pages, it is a good idea to protect the surrounding areas with newspaper or cloth, wear protective gloves – and a face mask when using wood bleach – and work in a well ventilated room.

Using Strippers

1 Using a bristle brush, apply a generous layer of stripper to your wood surface and allow it to sit until the paint or varnish begins to bubble.

2 Remove the softened paint or varnish with coarse steelwool. Wipe off excess stripper and remaining paint or varnish particles with a damp cloth and the neutralizer recommended by your product.

Cleaning Wax and Dirt

1 Dip fine steelwool into the proprietary furniture cleaner (see p. 11). Rub all over the wood. Do not allow the steelwool to get dry while rubbing.

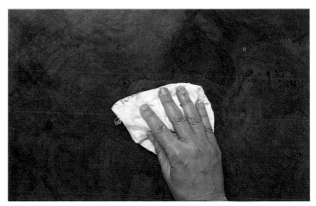

2 Wipe off the now loosened wax or dirt with a clean, dry cloth. You can reapply the cleaner to any remaining traces of wax or dirt.

Removing Stubborn Stains

1 *Rub over your surface with fine steelwool dipped in proprietary furniture cleaner.*

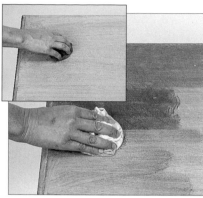

2 *The cleaner softens old wax and dirt and can make your surface appear white (inset). Wipe off the now loosened wax or dirt with a clean, dry cloth.*

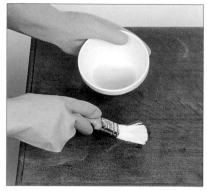

3 *Apply wood bleach using a vegetable-fiber brush which will not be destroyed by the bleach. If you do not have a vegetable-fiber brush use a cotton cloth. Allow the bleach to dry.*

4 *When the surface is dry, you will be able to see if any stains remain. If so, reapply the bleach to the stained areas. When you are satisfied, apply the manufacturer's recommended neutralizer using a clean cloth (inset), and then wash over it with water. Here, the oily stains on the left of the table are completely removed.*

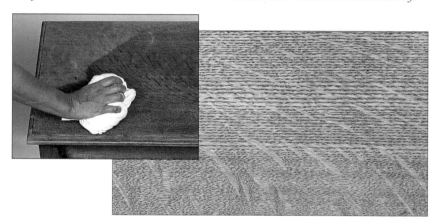

Removing Oil Marks

1 *After Cleaning Wax and Dirt (see p. 13), cover oil marks with fuller's earth powder. The powder absorbs the oil, drawing it out of the wood.*

2 *After 6 hours, the powder can be removed using a vacuum cleaner or bristle brush.*

3 *Using a stiff bristle brush, remove the last traces of powder. If the oil mark is not completely removed – as here – the process can be repeated.*

Resticking Veneers

1 To rejoin veneer that is peeling from the surface, first press down one side of the veneer with your fingers to check that it is still flexible and will not crack. If it does crack, the gap will need to be filled (see below).

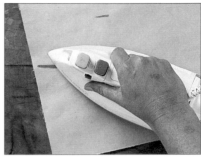

2 Cover the loose veneer with brown paper and press down on it with a hot iron until the old glue backing is sufficiently heated and the two sides stick back together again.

Fixing Gaps in Veneers

1 If the edge between two pieces of veneer is too far apart you need to fix it using a hard sealing wax, which comes in stick form. Use a wax that is slightly darker than the wood. First, using steelwool, rub a thin layer of ordinary dark wax into the surface to protect it from the hot wax you are going to add next.

2 Using a lighter, melt the sealing wax stick directly over the gap so that drips of wax fall into it.

3 Use a palette knife to press the softened hot wax into the gaps (near right). You may want to use a hair dryer to keep the wax pliable and easy to mold.

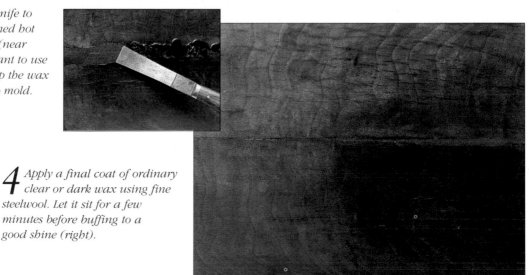

4 Apply a final coat of ordinary clear or dark wax using fine steelwool. Let it sit for a few minutes before buffing to a good shine (right).

Types of Wood

THERE ARE MANY SOURCES of furniture or wooden objects on which to use the techniques featured in this book. Secondhand furniture stores provide a rich source of old wood for decoration. New pine, since it is a fast-growing wood, is available cheaply almost everywhere and mass production, where cheap woods are faced with veneers (thin slivers of finer wood), ensures an almost endless supply of furniture. Woods such as walnut, cherry, bird's eye maple, and yew are rarer and more expensive, but they are frequently available as less expensive veneers. Increasingly woods from Africa (see p. 19) are becoming available as an alternative to the dwindling supplies of hardwoods from rainforest areas.

Old Secondhand Woods

Older woods are generally darker than new ones, due to the natural aging process. You will find secondhand pieces in mahogany, pine, walnut, and oak. You can use old woods for all the techniques demonstrated in this book, although they are better suited to the techniques that brighten the surface and so provide more contrast. Try Painting and Distressing *(see pp. 44–47),* Bleaching *(see p. 65–67), and* Liming *(see p. 77).*

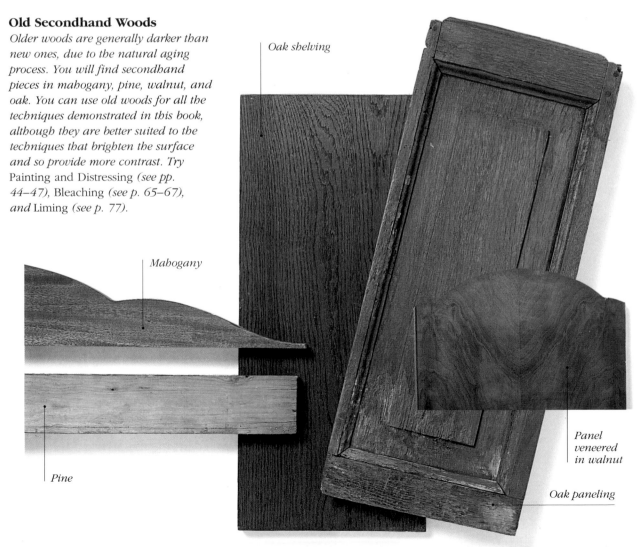

Oak shelving

Mahogany

Pine

Panel veneered in walnut

Oak paneling

Newly Cut Woods

Newly cut woods tend to be light in color like pine, which is slightly yellow. Pine is the most readily available wood because it grows quickly and easily and is fairly inexpensive. You can use newly cut woods for all the techniques in this book, although they are better suited to the techniques that darken the surface and so provide more contrast. Try Using Homemade Stains, Modern Stains *(see pp. 52–61), and* Fuming *(see p. 63).* Penwork *(see pp. 68–71) works very well on satinwood.*

Mahogany

Oak

Oak lampbase

Plywood bowl

Ash frame

Oak flooring

Pine carved bracket

Beech leg

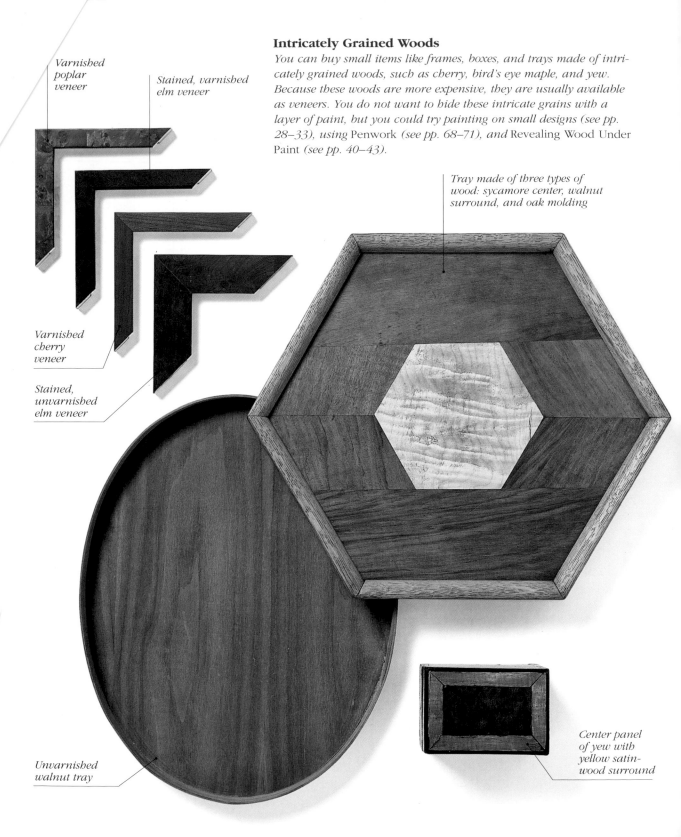

Intricately Grained Woods

You can buy small items like frames, boxes, and trays made of intricately grained woods, such as cherry, bird's eye maple, and yew. Because these woods are more expensive, they are usually available as veneers. You do not want to hide these intricate grains with a layer of paint, but you could try painting on small designs (see pp. 28–33), using Penwork (see pp. 68–71), and Revealing Wood Under Paint (see pp. 40–43).

Varnished poplar veneer

Stained, varnished elm veneer

Varnished cherry veneer

Stained, unvarnished elm veneer

Tray made of three types of wood: sycamore center, walnut surround, and oak molding

Unvarnished walnut tray

Center panel of yew with yellow satinwood surround

Exotic Woods

In recent years, awareness of the way in which slow-growing hardwoods are felled in forests all over the world has caused us to look elsewhere for supplies. Woods from Africa have been introduced to try to meet the demand caused by the loss of woods from rainforest areas. African woods – like redwood, cedar, iroko, and zebrawood – tend to have dramatic color changes in their grain, from warm yellows to strong browns and deep reds. Because of their strong color and pattern it may be better to use a plainer technique on these woods. Try Using Homemade *or* Modern Stains *(see pp. 52–61) to bring out the grain, or* Painting and Distressing *(see pp. 44–47), using a cool shade of paint.*

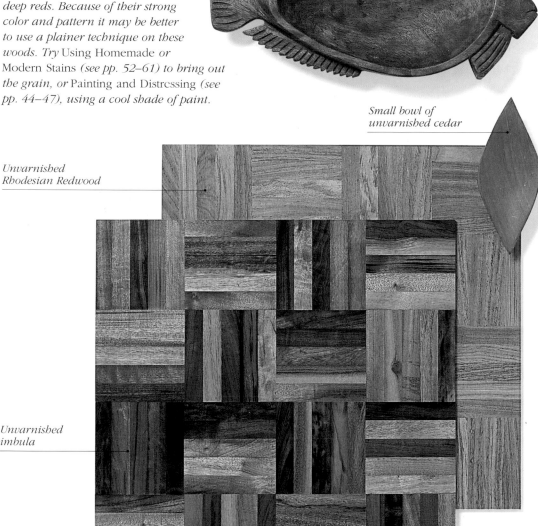

Dark cedar tray
from Tahiti

Small bowl of
unvarnished cedar

Unvarnished
Rhodesian Redwood

Unvarnished
imbula

Light cedar spindle

Varnishes, Oils, and Waxes

V ARNISHES, OILS, AND WAXES protect the surface of decorated wood and give it a sheen and a finished look. There are two types of varnish that particularly suit wood finishes because of the tone of color they impart: shellac and oil-base varnish. Shellac is also called French, Button, or Garnet Polish, depending on its depth of color which varies from deep brown to almost clear amber. Oil-base varnishes give a slightly yellowish appearance to the wood and are available in flat, middle-sheen, and gloss finishes. Water-base varnishes do not look as effective on decorated wood since it lacks depth and can leave a plastic film over the surface. Water-base varnish can only be used over sealed wood (see p. 12).

Shellac

Although shellac is not a strong varnish and water will mark it easily, it is very useful since it is so quick-drying. You can use it over wax, making it a useful finish for Painting and Distressing *(see pp. 44–47), and create a high sheen with shellac by applying several coats. To make shellac stronger and more resilient, you can apply a coat of wax or oil-base varnish over it.*

Untreated pine

Untreated mahogany

Untreated mahogany

Wax stencil and colored wax on pine with shellac finish

Oil-base stain in black and mahogany-red on mahogany with shellac finish

Plain mahogany with shellac finish

Oil-Base Varnishes

Oil-base varnishes are strong and hard-wearing. They take about six hours to dry. A glossy oil-base varnish gives the shiniest finish, so use them over Penwork *(see pp. 68–71),* Painting and Embellishing Wood *(see pp. 28–33), and* Woodgraining *(see pp. 34–39), which all need a slightly glossy look to help bring the work to life.*

APPLYING VARNISH

1 *Use a good quality flat-ended, soft-haired varnish brush. Load the brush with varnish, keeping it at a low angle and spreading the varnish thinly over the surface.*

2 *Feather out the varnish by holding the brush at right angles to the surface. This spreads the varnish so that it is as thin as possible and not likely to drip.*

Untreated pine

Untreated pine

Untreated mahogany

Pen and ink on pine with glossy oil-base varnish finish

Hand painting on pine with glossy oil-base varnish finish

Plain mahogany with glossy oil-base varnish finish

Oils generally give the flattest look of all and you can apply them to woods as an alternative to the more usual waxes and varnishes. There are many different oils on the market, such as Tung oil, Danish oil, and Teak oil. Tung oil, sometimes called Chinese wood oil, is particularly hard-wearing (it is resistant to water, alcohol, and food acids) and weather-resistant, so you can use it indoors and outdoors. Oil finishes are colorless over light woods, but will make dark woods appear even darker.

Wax is an age-old finish for wood, and makes it slightly waterproof with a mellow sheen. You can buy waxes in many colors from mahogany-reds and near-blacks to yellow tones.

Oil Finishes

You generally rub oils into wood with a cloth rather than a brush. You can use oils over a modern painted design (see pp. 28–33) or over the flat, water-base, pale-colored stains (see pp. 56–61), which need the flatter, more mellow look of an oil finish. For a soft sheen, apply a final coat of wax. Check the manufacturer's instructions to make sure that the particular oil will work over water-base paints and stains.

Untreated pine

Untreated pine

Untreated mahogany

Water-base stain on pine with oil finish

Plain pine with oil finish

Hand painting on mahogany with oil finish

Wax

For a soft sheen, which has a slight shine and a mellowing effect on the work, you can use clear, dark, or colored wax. It is not completely waterproof and so is best suited to interior use, away from water. You can apply wax over most bases, but it will remove paint if you apply it with excessive force.

APPLYING WAX

1 Apply a generous amount of wax with the finest-grade steelwool, working the wax well into the wood, both across and with the grain. Allow the wax to evaporate until it is no longer wet to the touch.

2 Using a polishing brush or a clean cloth, buff the surface to a soft sheen.

Untreated pine

Untreated mahogany

Untreated mahogany

Water-base paint on pine with clear wax finish

Homemade stain on mahogany with clear wax finish

Plain mahogany with dark wax finish

Paint on Wood

& Co. LTD.
8 5DF
105

Tools and Materials

Fine artist's brushes (no's 0 to 4 sable or sable mixtures are best)

Pencil

Aᴺʏ ᴡᴀᴛᴇʀ-ʙᴀsᴇ ᴘᴀɪɴᴛs, also known as acrylic paints, can be used when painting on wood and it is important to use good quality brushes, especially when doing intricate hand painting. Working with a brush that does not have a good point or is loose will result in poor work since the brush is not controllable. Techniques that use paint on wood include hand painting and stenciling designs which can then be embellished using metal leaf. Other techniques involve imitating a wood grain with brushes, combs, and graining rollers, revealing wood under a painted surface, or distressing the painted wood using wax and steelwool.

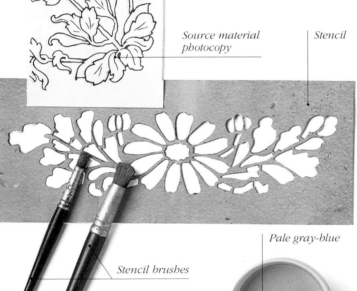

Source material photocopy

Stencil

Water-base Paints

ʙᴇʟᴏᴡ *There is a basic range of traditional colors used for painting on wood. The colors tend to be biased toward cool blues and greens as a foil to the warmth of the wood. Spots of warm pink, pale orange, off-white, and creamy ocher could also be used.*

Stencil brushes

Painting Designs on Wood

ᴀʙᴏᴠᴇ *Collect pictures of possible designs for transferring onto your surface, taking inspiration from old painted furniture and designs found on fabric and china. Use fine artist's brushes, no's 0 to 4 sable or sable mixtures, for painting intricate designs on wood, and stencil brushes when stenciling on wood (see pp. 28–33).*

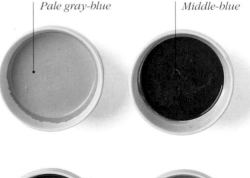

Pale gray-blue

Middle-blue

Warm raspberry-pink

Gray-green

Middle-green

Pale terra-cotta

Woodgraining

BELOW AND RIGHT There are speciality tools you can buy for
Woodgraining *(see pp. 34–39), but some of these can be
improvized at home. Combs, for example, can be made
from plastic tiles, and household brushes can be used
instead of a flogging or dragging brush. However, the
speciality transparent water-base glaze is essential. When
this is mixed with paint it gives it a translucent quality
and stops it from drying out, giving you more time to
complete the technique.*

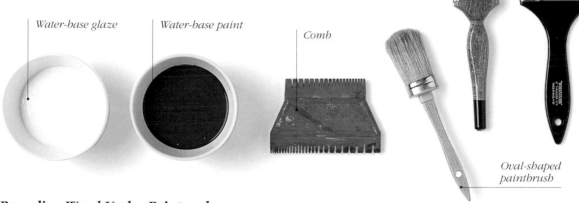

*Flogging brush (a
dragging brush can
also be used)*

*Flat-ended
paintbrush*

Water-base glaze

Water-base paint

Comb

*Oval-shaped
paintbrush*

Revealing Wood Under Paint and
Painting and Distressing

*BELOW Use paint stripper to reveal wood under a painted
finish or masking fluid as a variation (see pp. 40–43).
To achieve a distressed effect, rub your surface with wax
before painting over it, then rub away the paint in places
using steelwool. Crackleglaze can also be used to create
a similar, antiqued effect (see pp. 44–47).*

Applying Metal Leaf

*BELOW Another way to embellish wood is by
Applying Metal Leaf (see p. 32). Metal leaf, here
Dutch metal leaf which imitates gold, is not as
expensive as it might look. It is applied with
a special glue called gold size.*

*Crackleglaze
medium*

*Masking
fluid*

Gold size

*Fine
steelwool*

*Paint
stripper*

Clear wax

*Dutch
metal leaf*

*Small bristle brush
for applying size*

Painting and Embellishing Wood

Embellished Container
The varnish was removed from this small container, which was then hand painted in white, red, and blue water-base paint. The red is used as the underlying color on the painted basket, to give richness and liveliness to the design.

PAINTED DESIGNS ON WOOD, usually of flowers, leaves, and fruit, were especially popular in Britain in the 18th century, and often parts of the surface were also covered with metal leaf (see p. 32) for added decoration. To paint designs on wood you can use either tracing or stencils. The first method gives a more authentic hand-painted look but requires greater confidence. Painted designs work well on smooth, finely-grained woods since coarse-grained woods can be too textured – pale, yellow woods like satinwood are a favorite choice. For best results, seal the wood surface using sanding sealer before decorating (see p. 12).

TOOLS & MATERIALS

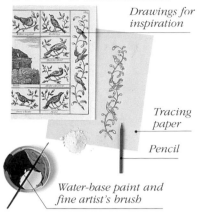

Drawings for inspiration

Tracing paper

Pencil

Water-base paint and fine artist's brush

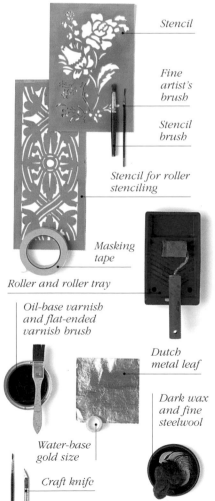

Stencil

Fine artist's brush

Stencil brush

Stencil for roller stenciling

Masking tape

Roller and roller tray

Oil-base varnish and flat-ended varnish brush

Dutch metal leaf

Dark wax and fine steelwool

Water-base gold size

Craft knife

Soft-haired brush

The Basic Technique

1 Trace a design using tracing paper and a pencil. You can buy books which contain copyright-free designs to work from.

2 For a light wood, rub a dark pigment or pencil onto the back of the design; for a dark wood, use pale-colored chalk or pigment.

3 Turn the tracing paper over and position on the wood. With a sharp pencil, draw over the design again.

4 The design shows up as a delicate line. Using water-base paint, paint the outline of your design. Use a darker paint – here, a dark green – to fill in the design (inset).

5 Use a lighter color to highlight parts of the design (inset). If in doubt about where to add the pale color, follow the convention of highlighting the left-hand side, as if the light is falling from above and left.

Embellishing a Stencil with Hand Painting

You can use a stencil as the base for hand painting. Once you have applied the stencil, you can either add light hand painting, applying spots and lines, or you can blend the separate shapes of the stencil by painting over its bridges – the solid strips of the stencil which hold it together.

1 Secure your stencil in place using repositioning glue/Spray Mount or masking tape. Put a very little water-base paint on a small stencil brush.

2 Apply paint by wiping or dabbing the brush. Add more paint to some areas – here, the center of the flower – for a three-dimensional effect.

3 Partly remove the stencil to check that the paint has gone on as required and add more paint in some areas if necessary.

4 When the paint is dry, rub over the design with very fine steelwool to create a smooth finish.

5 Using a fine artist's brush, hand paint lines in dark green to define the rib and veins of the leaves.

6 Use a paler color on the edges to highlight the design, and give it a three-dimensional look.

7 Hand paint extra petals (inset). Work over the whole stencil to create a hand-painted effect.

Stenciling a Floor

1 Mark the edges of your border with masking tape on the whole floor then position the stencil using repositioning glue/Spray Mount or masking tape. Work a sponge roller through a little water-base paint, removing any excess, then apply to the stencil.

2 Remove the stencil and place it at the next position so that the design matches up and slightly overlaps. Continue stenciling across the whole floor.

3 When you have completed the whole floor, allow it to dry and then remove the masking tape around the border edges.

4 To frame the design in a different color, position a straight line of masking tape on top of the border and another line of tape below it. Paint in between the two masking tape lines with your contrasting color.

5 When the whole floor is dry, remove the masking tape lines to display two bands of color on either side of the border. To protect the floor, apply a coat of shellac or oil-base varnish (see pp. 20–21).

Applying Metal Leaf

Metallic finishes, usually gold in color, have long been used to decorate carved wood. You cover the wooden background in loose metal leaf, leaving the carving standing proud. Metal leaf – here, loose Dutch metal leaf which imitates gold – is applied using a special glue called gold size.

2 Apply the loose metal leaf, which sticks immediately to the gold size. Use a soft-haired brush to dab the sheets down well and remove any excess leaf from intricate areas.

1 First seal the wood (see p. 12). Paint all around the wooden motif using water-base gold size. Let stand for 10–15 minutes until the size is clear and tacky.

3 Use a craft knife to cut away any larger pieces of metal leaf around the edges of the motif. If you have missed any areas, add more size and apply the metal leaf again.

4 Using a flat-ended, soft-haired varnish brush, apply a dark shellac or oil-base varnish (see pp. 20–21) to the entire wood and metal leaf surface. Allow the varnish to dry.

5 Using fine steelwool, apply a coat of dark wax over the motif and where the metal leaf and wood meet. Allow to dry for about 5 minutes.

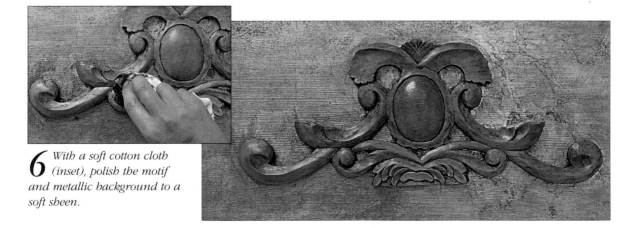

6 With a soft cotton cloth (inset), polish the motif and metallic background to a soft sheen.

Decorated Bedside Cabinet

RIGHT *This walnut-veneered bedside cabinet was stenciled with a garland and wreath design and hand painted.*

COLOR COMBINATIONS

Greens on oak

Browns on mahogany

Deep reds on pitch pine

Blues on sycamore

Garlanded Chair

ABOVE *This chair was decorated with "Morning Glory" entwined around the legs and garlands of roses and leaves on the back. A row of pearl-like balls, hand-painted light blue dots, was used across the central chair slat. On each ball a dot of brighter paint gives a three-dimensional quality (detail above chair).*

Hand-painted Piano Stool

ABOVE *This mahogany piano stool was hand painted in water-base paint with a posy and garland (detail above stool). The bright colors show clearly against the dark wood.*

Woodgraining

Woodgrained Mirror
The plain pine wood of this frame was enhanced using the Bird's Eye Maple *technique (see opposite). The brush has created a curly grain by twisting the glaze like locks of hair and the darker patches were created using pigment.*

IN THE PAST, OBJECTS MADE OF pine were always painted because this knotty, yellow wood was considered commonplace. For this technique, you apply a colored water-base glaze and pull a comb or speciality grainer through it, or mark it with a brush to imitate the grain of wood. An oak effect is particularly good for sturdy household items, but for more decorative pieces a fancy wood such as bird's eye maple, walnut, or mahogany might be imitated. Vinegar painting is an alternative, cheaper method. The graining achieved is more fanciful and not necessarily faithful to a particular wood. Woodgraining adds elegance and a sense of solidity to a piece of furniture and is best used on inexpensive, less interesting woods. For best results, seal the wood surface before decorating (see p. 12).

TOOLS & MATERIALS

Tray with brush for mixing and transparent water-base glaze

Raw umber pigment

Raw sienna water-base paint

Flat-ended paintbrush

Flogging brush (or use a dragging brush)

Graduated and triangular combs

Graining roller

Cotton cloth

Neutral wax and fine steelwool for applying it

Water-base paint

Vinegar

Feather

Mounting putty/ Blu-Tack

The Basic Technique: Bird's Eye Maple

Mix the glaze and paint a bit at a time so that the color varies slightly from batch to batch as it does in real wood. The ratio is usually 4 parts water-base glaze (see p. 27) to 1 part water-base paint, but you can add more glaze to increase the transparency of the mixture.

1 Mix the glaze well with raw sienna paint and raw umber pigment to achieve a shade similar to maple. Test the translucency of the mixture on spare wood if possible.

2 Load a wide, flat-ended paintbrush with the mixture. Holding it as shown, pull the brush down, applying pressure at intervals and angling it to make the grainy lines curve.

3 Dab the tip of a clean, flat-ended brush onto places where the glaze is thickest to create a textured effect.

4 Where the glaze is thick, make small dots – "bird's eyes" – in the wet glaze with the end of your finger.

5 The finished effect is a mixture of dark- and light-colored glaze with grain lines and "bird's eyes." When the glaze is dry, apply a coat of water- or oil-base varnish. The latter helps to create the look of old wood.

The Basic Technique: Oak Graining

This technique uses different types of combs – triangular and graduated – to make different widths of painted lines to create the appearance of the wood's grain. Although it is called oak graining here, you can also use this technique to imitate mahogany or any other straight-lined wood.

1 Mix water-base glaze with dark brown and deep red water-base paint (about 4 parts glaze to 1 part paint). Using a flat-ended paintbrush, apply the glaze thinly.

2 Use a rubber comb – a triangular one has three sides with different teeth widths, of which the finest and medium are most useful. Pull down the fine-toothed comb to make a striped grain, through which you can see the underlying grain of the wood.

3 Pull down a graduated comb, which has teeth varying from wide to narrow, next to the first grain. Use medium, fine-toothed, and graduated combs randomly next to each other.

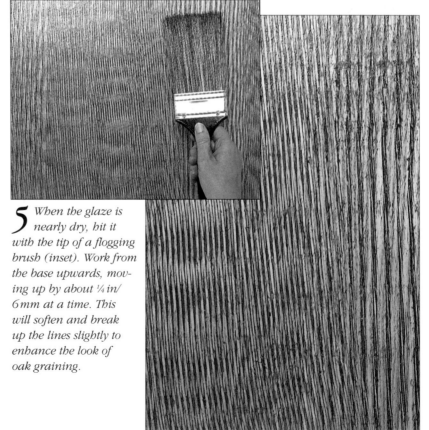

5 When the glaze is nearly dry, hit it with the tip of a flogging brush (inset). Work from the base upwards, moving up by about ¼ in/ 6 mm at a time. This will soften and break up the lines slightly to enhance the look of oak graining.

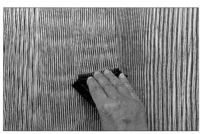

4 With the fine teeth of the triangular comb, pull down at a slight angle over the lines already made. Do this only once or twice in an area 3¼ ft/1 m wide.

Using a Graining Roller

Graining rollers come in rubber or plastic. You use them in one direction to create the look of pine and in the other direction to create the look of oak.

For successful results, first seal the surface (see p. 12), keep the roller moving, and only apply a small amount of paint and glaze to the surface.

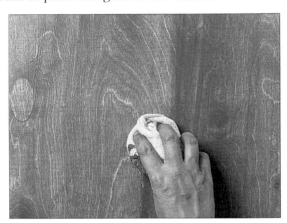

2 Using a cotton cloth, gently wipe over the wet glaze surface in the direction of the grain, removing some of the glaze so that only a very fine film remains and the wood underneath shows through.

1 Mix 4 parts water-base glaze to 1 part water-base paint. With a flat-ended paintbrush apply the glaze evenly in the direction of the grain.

3 Hold the roller with the ridges curving upward (inset) to make a fine, slim, pine grain. Position the roller on the surface with the cylinder a quarter of the way down. Pull and gently roll the cylinder halfway down its length without stopping. This may require practice. Continue rolling from top to bottom.

4 Hold the roller with the ridges curving down (inset) to make a wide, broad, oak grain. Pull and roll down the surface as in Step 3. For a natural look, the long oval shapes in the effect should fall in different positions on each vertical line. Use combs in between the roller finish for a random effect.

PITFALLS

Take care to use a thin layer of glaze when graining. If you apply the glaze and paint mixture too thickly, the result will be unnatural and may look textured when dry (near right). If the effect looks opaque (far right), you are using too much paint, so add more glaze. Wherever possible, test for translucency on spare wood.

Glaze mixture is too thick

Too much paint in mixture

Vinegar Painting

This technique uses household materials – here, mounting putty/Blu-Tack – to imitate wood. A wax base ensures that the paint and vinegar mix dries slowly, giving you time to decorate the surface. Experiment with the paint mixture, adding more vinegar, a little at a time, until the mix adheres.

1 Using fine steelwool, work neutral or clear wax into the surface of the wood. Allow the solvent in the wax to evaporate for 5 minutes.

2 Mix any variety of vinegar with water-base paint (about 1 part vinegar to 1 part paint) and stir well. The mixture should have a translucent quality.

3 With a flat-ended paintbrush, apply the mixture onto the waxed surface. It may resist the solution at first, so keep brushing until the paint covers it.

4 Take a small piece of mounting putty/Blu-Tack and form it into a ball, arch, or simple twisted shape. Experiment to see what shape it makes when printed.

5 The wax base makes the paint take longer to dry than normal. Press down on the surface of the paint with the mounting putty/Blu-Tack which lifts off paint so you can see the base beneath. Reform the mounting putty/Blu-Tack when it becomes covered in paint. Allow the paint to dry, then coat with oil-base varnish or shellac (see p. 21).

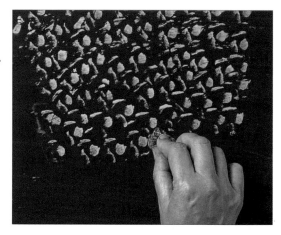

ALTERNATIVES

You can use any long, strong feather – such as goose or duck – to make other designs. Fan the feather into an arch shape or push and lift it alternately as here (near right). You can also make interesting patterns using your fingers and fingertips (far right).

Using a feather

Using your fingers

Grained and Combed Cupboard

ABOVE This small pine cupboard has a blue combed finish created using both the graining roller and a graduated comb.

Woodgrained Door

BELOW The grain of this old pine door was enhanced to give it a richer, more elegant finish, with a reddish bird's eye maple effect in the panel. Brown glaze was combed and dragged on the stiles and rails. The molding had a thin comb dragged down it.

Vinegar-painted Chair

LEFT AND BELOW A mix of 1 part vinegar to 1 part brown water-base paint was applied to this pine chair. An eraser was used to decorate the slats and fingertips were dabbed onto other parts.

COLOR COMBINATIONS

Red-brown on pine

Light green-blue on pine

Dark green on pine

White on pine

Revealing Wood Under Paint

Y OU CAN USE PAINT STRIPPER or masking fluid to strip away parts of a solidly painted surface to expose the underlying wood. Because paint stripper removes paint, you can use it to draw a pattern on paint to reveal the wood underneath. Or you can apply masking fluid in a pattern and paint over it when dry. The dried masking fluid prevents the paint from reaching the wood. When the paint is dry, you peel off the masking fluid to reveal the unpainted wood. Because these techniques reveal small sections of wood, they are best for embellishing pieces that have a regular, pronounced, or closely repeating grain – pine, ash, or oak, for example.

Painted and Revealed Table

This plain oak table was painted with a deep blue oil-base paint. Then using a design based on an old piece of Swiss painted furniture, paint stripper was used to reveal the oak underneath. The contrasting textures of the flat, solid paint and the newly revealed grain of the wood gives this effect its appeal.

TOOLS & MATERIALS

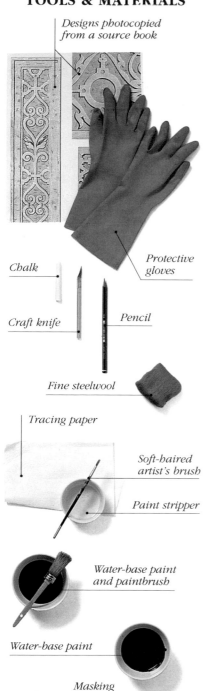

Designs photocopied from a source book

Protective gloves

Chalk

Craft knife

Pencil

Fine steelwool

Tracing paper

Soft-haired artist's brush

Paint stripper

Water-base paint and paintbrush

Water-base paint

Masking fluid

The Basic Technique

1 *Apply water- or oil-base paint over a sealed surface (see p. 12). Start at Step 2 if you are working on a previously painted surface.*

2 *Using chalk, draw out your design on the paint. It should not be too intricate. Alternatively, use the tracing method (see p. 42).*

3 *Using an old, soft-haired artist's brush, cover your chalk lines with paint stripper. Keep applying until the paint becomes moist and blisters.*

4 *Before it dries out, blot the design with absorbent paper to soak up any excess paint stripper. You may need to do a large design in sections.*

5 *Using fine steelwool and wearing protective gloves, rub over the areas where you applied paint stripper (inset), until all the paint is removed. To stop the reaction, carefully wipe these areas with water.*

Stripper has not removed all paint *Stripper left on wrong area of paint*

Using Masking Fluid

Masking fluid is a pale yellow liquid, which dries to a rubberlike consistency. It is frequently used by watercolorists, but many craftspeople also use it to mask out areas. When doing this technique, wash out your brush in warm water immediately after use, so the fluid does not dry on the brush.

1 *Trace a design from a source book, in this case a wood carving. Choose a simple design that has bold shapes and works well in silhouette.*

2 *To transfer the design, rub the back of the paper with dark or light pigment or pencil. Then turn the paper over and draw over the original pencil lines onto the wood.*

3 *Using an artist's brush, paint generously inside the design with masking fluid. If you make a mistake, wipe it off immediately.*

4 *When the fluid is dry it will be a dark yellow. Paint over it with either water-base paint, which dries quickly, or more slow-drying oil-base paint. Allow to dry.*

5 *Peel off the masking fluid. You may need to use a craft knife to lift off the dried fluid, but take care not to scratch the paintwork.*

6 *The final result shows the grain of the wood contrasting well with the flat quality of the paint. Here, the striped grain of the wood is echoed by the linear nature of the design.*

Blue and Brown Chair

LEFT AND BELOW This chair was already painted dark brown. When it was decorated with paint stripper, a blue paint was discovered underneath, which shows through in places, making an interesting color combination of dark and light brown and blue.

COLOR COMBINATIONS

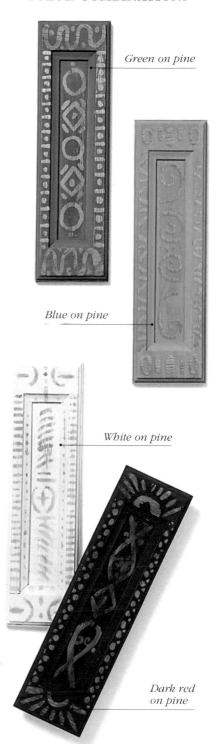

Green on pine

Blue on pine

White on pine

Dark red on pine

Decorative Panel

RIGHT This panel was decorated using paint stripper on a previously painted box. The pattern was based on an old stencil design. The different textures of the wood, which has a fairly plain grain, and the paint offer considerable interest.

Patterned Eggcups

ABOVE These new, varnished eggcups were given their bold individual patterns using masking fluid. Each cup was decorated in a different color, using water-base paint. They were then varnished again to seal the surface, making them safe for use with food and washable.

Painting and Distressing

THIS TECHNIQUE, SOMETIMES called wax resist, relies on the fact that oil and water do not mix: you apply water-base paint over a solvent-based wax and, as long as the solvent does not evaporate, you can easily rub away the paint with steelwool for a distressed effect. Alternatively, a crackleglaze medium will also give an antiqued finish. In the past this technique appeared on pine, which was considered too plain to be left unpainted. You can do it on any wood, but it is best suited to closely grained woods since you only reveal small sections of the grain at a time.

Painted and Distressed Chair

This classic chair was painted with an off-white water-base paint over soft wax, focusing on areas where there would have been wear and tear. The paint remained in the recesses and was removed from the raised areas.

TOOLS & MATERIALS

Solvent-based wax

Fine steelwool

Water-base paint and paintbrush for applying it

Coarse steelwool

Household candle

Water-base paint

Water-base varnish and flat-ended, varnish brush

Crackleglaze medium and paint-brush

The Basic Technique

1 Apply wax to the wood with fine steelwool in random patches, as if paint has worn away in places. Apply clear or neutral wax if using a pale-colored paint.

2 The wax will harden a little, but do not let it dry out completely. Cover the whole area, both wood and wax, with water-base paint. Allow to dry thoroughly.

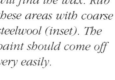

3 The paint appears darker where you will find the wax. Rub these areas with coarse steelwool (inset). The paint should come off very easily.

PITFALLS

If the paint is wet when you rub it with steelwool, it will spread over the wood, leaving a lightly painted area, rather than clear patches. Do not rub too vigorously on the waxed areas, or you may rub paint back into the wood.

Using a Candle

1 You can also use candlewax for distressing. Rub the candle on the wood in patches, using considerable pressure to make an impression.

2 Candlewax does not need to dry out. Paint over it immediately with water-base paint. Allow to dry.

3 Using coarse steelwool, rub the waxed areas. Since candlewax is not very greasy, these sections may be less obvious than they are in The Basic Technique (see p. 45).

Using Crackleglaze

1 Over several coats of sanding sealer (see p. 12), apply a water-base varnish.

2 Apply crackleglaze medium to the wood. Use several coats of the medium to achieve very large cracks.

3 When dry, cover with slightly diluted water-base paint. Do not overwork the paint, but simply lay down each brushstroke. After a few minutes, cracks will appear. A more diluted paint will give large, more open, and slightly translucent areas (inset).

Crackleglazed Plant Pedestal
ABOVE *A pine pedestal was given two layers of varnish and two layers of crackleglaze medium. A coat of dark red water-base paint was then applied. Some areas had more diluted paint applied to it, giving a very light look.*

Wax Resist Frame

ABOVE This pine frame was marked with a design using a candle. The frame was painted dark red and the waxed areas were rubbed with steelwool to reveal the decorative pattern.

Stenciled Green Cupboard

BELOW A dark solvent-based wax was stenciled onto this old pine kitchen cabinet. Dark green paint was painted over the whole piece and the stenciled areas were rubbed with steelwool to reveal the pattern.

COLOR COMBINATIONS

Gray on pine

Bright blue on pine

Brown on pine

Pale blue on pine

Distressed Corner Cupboard

ABOVE Blue paint was applied over clear wax and the waxed areas were rubbed with steelwool to give a very heavily distressed look.

Stains on Wood

Tools and Materials

ALL TYPES OF STAIN change the color of wood by penetrating the grain, rather than resting on the surface. You can easily make your own stains by mixing pigments, ferrous sulfate, or Van Dyck crystals with water, or you can use the precolored water- and oil-base stains available from hardware stores.

There are other techniques for staining wood. The fumes of ammonia carbonate act on the tannin in wood and penetrate it, making it darker (see p. 63). To lighten wood, you can use a simple bleaching technique which calls for two solutions, used one after another (see p. 65).

Inks also stain a wood surface. The ink penetrates the wood, rather than sitting on the surface like paint. Drawing ink has a deep, rich color but ordinary writing ink, although of a thinner quality, can also be used.

Homemade Stains

BELOW Van Dyck crystals, ferrous sulfate – available from hardware or speciality stores – and pigments – available from art supply stores – can all be mixed with water to make your own stains of varying strengths (see pp. 52–55).

Ferrous sulfate

Brown pigment

Yellow pigment

Red pigment

Van Dyck crystals

Oil-base Stains

BELOW Oil-base stains are usually available in brown wood colors. The stain penetrates the wood and tends to run along the grain easily. When making a design with stain, use a sharp craft knife to incise the wood and prevent the stain from flowing along the grain. Use a metal ruler to guide the craft knife when staining symmetrical designs (see p. 60).

Metal ruler

Craft knife

Oil-base stain

Water-base Stains

RIGHT Proprietary water-base stains are available from hardware stores. Unlike oil-base stains, water-base stains are available in a wide range of bright colors which can be used to create a modern effect.

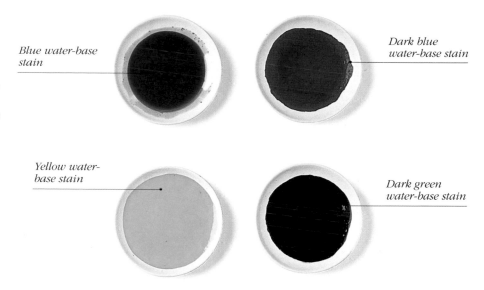

Blue water-base stain

Dark blue water-base stain

Yellow water-base stain

Dark green water-base stain

Fuming and Bleaching

BELOW The fumes of ammonia carbonate make wood darker, which is why this technique is known as fuming. To lighten wood, you can buy a speciality wood bleach which comes in two parts and is neutralized according to the manufacturer's instructions. You may also find a three-part bleach where the third part is a neutralizer.

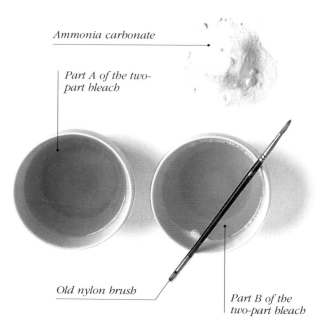

Ammonia carbonate

Part A of the two-part bleach

Old nylon brush

Part B of the two-part bleach

Penwork

BELOW Inks are another variety of stain, traditionally used with mapping pens and artist's brushes. Although black and sepia were the shades traditionally used, you can now buy inks in a much wider range of colors.

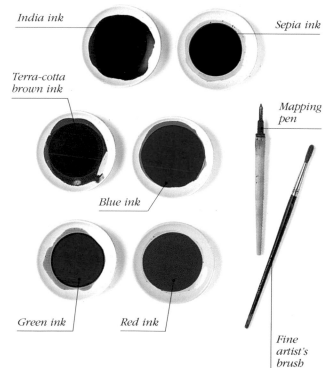

India ink

Sepia ink

Terra-cotta brown ink

Blue ink

Mapping pen

Green ink

Red ink

Fine artist's brush

Using Homemade Stains

Pigment-stained Birch Containers

These traditional Shaker-style birch pieces are stained using warmed pigment paste. A second color was applied to the edges and central areas of the tray.

I N THE PAST, WOOD HAS BEEN stained with many different materials. The easiest to use is a stain made with pigments, which is said to be the stain used by the Shakers. Van Dyck crystals (see p. 54) are still popular today for their richness of color, ease of use, and economy, and ferrous sulfate (see p. 54) also makes a useful and economical stain. The strength of your stain depends on the ratio you use of powder to water, but remember that soft, light wood generally changes color more readily than dark, harder wood. Stains are absorbed by wood and so work well to enhance the interesting, expansive grains of woods like walnut. These woods are usually expensive, but you can buy them as veneers at a fraction of the cost.

TOOLS & MATERIALS

Spoon

Pigment

Old saucepan

Cotton cloth

Van Dyck crystals

Van Dyck stain
and paintbrush

Protective
gloves

Ferrous
sulfate

The Basic Technique

Pigments come in varying strengths. The depth of color you obtain depends on the strength of your pigment and the type of wood you use. Experiment to find the ratio of pigment to water that you prefer.

1 Using an old saucepan (it will stain), add 1 part pigment to 5 parts water or your preferred ratio. Heat, stirring, until it begins to boil and has a thin, pastelike consistency.

2 Remove the saucepan from the heat and allow to cool slightly. Dip a cotton cloth into the mixture while still warm and rub well into the wood, using pressure.

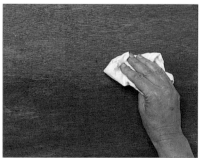

3 Using a clean cotton cloth, rub all over the surface to remove excess pigment. The grain of the wood should become increasingly apparent.

4 The surface should dry within a few minutes. If the color is not strong enough, apply a second coat of the warmed pigment paste.

5 With a dampened absorbent cloth, wipe over the surface again to remove all loose pigment.

Van Dyck Crystals

This is a rich brown staining medium bought in crystal form and dissolved in warm water. It was originally made from the soft outer husks of walnuts, but is now more likely to be made from an extract of peat bogs. The color depends on the strength of the stain, as shown on these pine blocks (right). These contain (left to right): 1 part Van Dyck crystals to 15 parts water; 1:10, 1:5, 1:2. A recommended strength is 1:5.

1:15   1:10   1:5   1:2

1 Wear protective gloves since the mixture is very strong and can stain the skin and nails. Combine 1 part Van Dyck crystals with 5 parts warm water. Mix well.

2 Apply a generous layer of stain to the wood. Do not allow it to dry in between strokes since any overlap may create darker areas.

3 Wipe off any excess stain using a clean dry cloth and allow the stain to dry completely.

Using Ferrous Sulfate

This is the chemical name for an iron compound that you can use to turn wood from gray to an inky-black, ebony color. It also turns oak silvery gray and gives walnut, which is naturally yellow, a gray tone. It only affects wood that contains tannin, such as oak, walnut, and sycamore.

1 For a very strong, dark stain, mix 1 part ferrous sulfate with 10 parts cold water and stir well. Test the mixture on a small, hidden area of your wood to judge the strength you require.

2 Paint on the stain and allow it to soak in. Here, it was painted on a piece of walnut. Wipe off any excess with a damp cloth (inset).

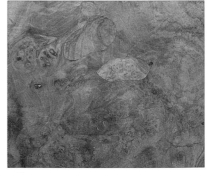

3 Here, the color of the wood has changed from a hot, almost orange color to a cooler gray-brown. It will have darker and lighter patches, depending on the grain of the wood.

COLOR COMBINATIONS

Red oxide on cherry

Blue and Green Stool

ABOVE Blue stain (1 part pigment to 5 parts water) was applied all over the stool using a cloth. When dry, green stain was applied using a brush around the edge of the seat.

Antwerp blue on maple

Banded Bed Headboard

BELOW 1 part ferrous sulfate to 20 parts water was painted in a band around the edge of this bed headboard, together with a thin, delicate line to emphasize its shape.

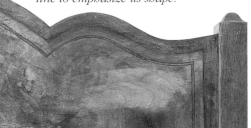

Stained Candlestick

ABOVE This oak candlestick was stripped of paint, leaving the wood looking dark, but dull. It was stained with Van Dyck crystals (1 part Van Dyck crystals to 5 parts water) to strengthen and warm it, leaving the raised bands in the original color.

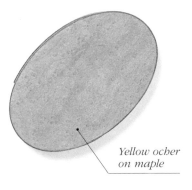

Yellow ocher on maple

PITFALLS

You must remove varnish from old pieces of furniture (see p. 13), or the stain will not reach the wood that is still covered by the varnish, as here. Carefully look at and feel the surface of your wood since varnished areas will be slightly shinier and smoother.

Burnt umber on birch

Using Modern Stains

THERE ARE TWO TYPES of modern stain, both of which are available ready-made from hardware stores and are relatively easy to use. Water-base stains come in bright, light, modern colors as well as wood colors. These stains work particularly well for soft woods and light-colored woods. Oil-base stains are available in mainly brown wood colors and produce strong, deeply penetrating stains, which work best with darker-colored woods. You can use modern stains on any wood to showcase its natural grain. You should bear in mind that the color of the wood will affect the eventual color of the stained work. A yellow wood, for instance, with a warm blue stain will result in a cool green-blue.

Stained Chair
This new pine chair was first stained in a raspberry-pink water-base stain. Over this a dark green stain was applied and then rubbed in places to reveal the pink (above). Several colors were used on the carved cockerel including red and ocher (right).

TOOLS & MATERIALS

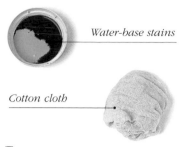

Water-base stains

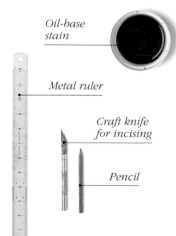

Cotton cloth

Bristle brush

Stencil brush

Stencil

Oil-base stain

Metal ruler

Craft knife for incising

Pencil

The Basic Technique

1 Using a bristle brush, apply water-base stain to the required areas. Don't worry if the colors appear bright; they will deaden when dry.

2 Rub off the excess stain with a clean, dry cotton cloth. Use a fresh piece of cloth for each area, so that you do not spread the stain.

3 Using a clean bristle brush, apply a second color of stain to other areas. If you are staining a carved object – as here – use a small brush so that you can reach into the crevices.

4 You can also apply color by dipping a cloth into some stain and wiping it over the raised areas. The cloth will not reach the recessed areas, creating a lively blend of colors.

5 Paint a coat of brown water-base stain over the surface to tone down the object. If you use a third coat, the stain will look dark and opaque. Varnish, wax, or oil the finished work (see pp. 20–23).

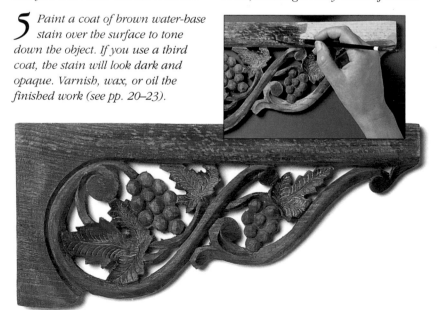

Using Two Colors

Here, the second color is applied in spots, but you can also apply a second color all over a stained surface to create a two-toned effect. Wood soaks up more stain in some areas than others so in some places the first color will be more apparent, and in others the second color will be dominant.

1 Rub all over the wood with medium-grade sandpaper. This breaks up the surface slightly, helping the stain to penetrate.

2 Wearing protective gloves, soak parts of a cotton cloth or sponge in the first stain – here, a water-base stain – then wipe it over the wood, following the direction of the grain. Avoid drips. Keep working into a wet edge to prevent two coats of stain from building up in any area, which would give a darker color.

3 Using a clean cloth, wipe off excess stain, again working in the direction of the grain. This will make the color of the wood appear lighter. Allow to dry for about 20 minutes.

4 Apply the second stain with a cloth or sponge, either in specific areas or all over. The two colors could contrast – here, green and red. Or, if the first color is bright, you can apply a muting color, such as brown or white.

5 Wipe off excess stain using a clean cloth, taking care to wipe the spots only, so that they do not smudge. Wiping off a lot of the second stain with considerable pressure will result in more of the first color being seen.

Stenciling with Stains

You can use water-base stains in the same way as paints to create patterns with stencils. Firmly attach the stencil to the surface using either masking tape or repositioning glue/Spray Mount. You want to be sure that stain can not seep underneath the stencil. You can stencil directly onto wood or onto stained work, but more than two layers of stain will become opaque.

1 The secret of stenciling with stains is to use a very small amount of stain on the brush. Dip a stencil brush in the liquid, dab it on some spare paper to remove the excess color and apply – here, to the flower.

2 Apply two or more colors to the rest of the stencil, using a clean stencil brush each time. Here, the different parts of the design were colored separately, but there could be more overlapping to create a blended effect.

3 To give depth, add a second color on top of the first in places. Here, we are adding to the flower center, but you could do it at the edge of the petals.

4 Lift up part of the stencil to check that the colors are working well and make any adjustments you consider necessary.

5 To give the stencil a coherent look, a little of the red and some blue was used on the leaves. With stenciling, which leaves a "gap" between parts of the design, you avoid the fuzzy edge created by painting colors back-to-back.

Making Patterns with Stains

To make a pattern using stains, you need to incise the wood with a craft knife. This prevents the stain from flowing along the grain and enables you to use two different colored stains side by side, without the risk of them spreading.

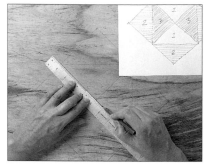

1 Draw your design on the wood using a pencil and ruler. Geometric patterns are easy to do.

2 Using a very sharp craft knife and a metal ruler, incise along the lines to a depth of 1/16 in/2 mm.

3 Using water- or oil-base stain, paint the design. Use a small bristle brush to reach the corners easily without spreading the stain. Use a larger bristle brush over bigger areas.

4 Apply a second color in the same way as the first. There is no need to wait for the first color to dry before doing this. You can then apply other colors in the same way. Protect the surface with a coat of varnish, oil, or wax on water-base stain or shellac on oil-base stain (see pp. 20–23).

Checkered Table

ABOVE *A geometric pattern with a three-dimensional effect was drawn and scored into this tabletop. Three shades of oil-base stain were then painted on using a small brush.*

Two-Tone Frame

ABOVE *This simple pine frame had a black oil-base stain applied using a small brush to part of the raised molding. A lighter oil-base stain was applied to the frame using a cloth.*

Stained Kitchen Cabinet Door

LEFT The color of the central panels was first deepened with diluted water-base stain. The stencil was then applied using the same stain at full strength. A black stain was applied to the molding.

COLOR COMBINATIONS

Plain, unstained beech

Blue water-base stain on beech

Swedish-Style Bench

BELOW AND RIGHT This new pine bench was stained using a water-base stain applied with a cloth. On the backrest a stencil was applied in water-base stains using stencil brushes.

Brown water-base stain on beech

Red water-base stain on beech

PITFALLS

Applying water-base stain can be tricky, especially over large areas, since the stain dries quickly. Wipe drips off quickly or they become impossible to remove, and try not to load the brush, cloth, or sponge with too much stain.

Fuming and Bleaching

FUMING AND BLEACHING are important techniques in the woodworker's repertoire. You fume wood to make it darker and bleach wood to make it lighter. To fume wood, allow the fumes from ammonia carbonate to act on the tannin content of wood giving it an aged look rather than simply a dark stain. Woods with a high tannin content, such as oak, walnut, and sycamore, respond well to fuming. Other woods will need to be coated in a strong tea solution. Consider the size of the object when fuming in relation to the size of the container you will need to fume it in.

To lighten dark woods, use a speciality two-part wood bleach (see p. 51). You can bleach a complete surface or selected areas to create a pattern. Some woods such as oak become yellow, while others such as mahogany become a little pink when bleached.

Fumed Frame

ABOVE Masking fluid (see p. 42) was applied in a leaf design on this small oak frame. The frame was then coated with tea and fumed overnight. The frame was finished with a coat of clear wax.

Bleached Box

RIGHT The inlaid mahogany panel and pine surrounds of this small box were incised and decorated using a two-part bleach. The box was finished with a coat of wax and polished to a soft sheen.

TOOLS & MATERIALS

Container for fuming. This can be made of any material

Bowl of ammonia carbonate

Plastic wrap for wrapping bowl

Strong black tea and paintbrush

Part A of two-part bleach and vegetable-fiber brush specially made for bleaches

Part B of two-part bleach

Neutralizer

Water

Face mask

Protective gloves

Cotton cloth

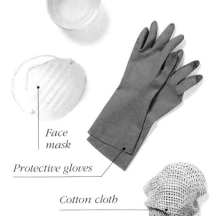

The Basic Technique: Fuming

The fumes from ammonia are very strong and can sting the eyes. Work in a well-ventilated area so that the fumes dissipate quickly and wear a face mask and goggles if preferred.

1 *Paint the wood with a strong tea solution made from 3 tea bags or 3 heaped teaspoons of loose tea to 1 cup of boiling water and left to brew for several hours.*

2 *Place the wood in a container – here, plastic – with a bowl of ammonia carbonate powder. Seal the container with a see-through covering such as plastic wrap.*

3 *After leaving for at least 12 hours, remove the object from your container. If it is not dark enough you can repeat Steps 1–3 using the same bowl of ammonia carbonate. After several uses the smell of the fumes will disappear. This is when you know the ammonia carbonate has lost its effectiveness.*

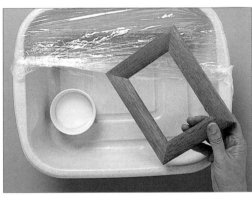

Fumed Frames
RIGHT *Parts of each frame were first masked before fuming. The outer frame was covered with torn strips of masking tape and the inner frame was painted in a pattern using masking fluid (see p. 42). Both masks were removed after fuming to reveal lighter decorative patterns.*

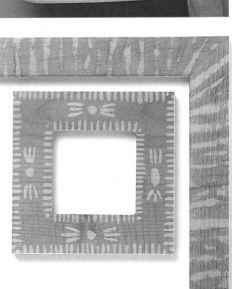

Fuming a Pattern

It is easy to fume a pattern on wood by using the tannin content of tea, especially on a wood that does not already have a high tannin content. Paint a strong solution of tea (see p. 63) inside a traced and incised design. Be sure to make enough tea to cover your whole design – 1 cup would be plenty for a small design. After fuming, the wood will appear darker where you have painted it with tea.

1 Trace in pencil a design that has large, bold shapes and is not too intricate. For a light wood, rub a dark pigment or pencil onto the back of the design; for a dark wood use pale-colored chalk or pigment.

2 Transfer the design to the wood by tracing over it again. Where you apply pressure, the pigment will leave a mark on the wood.

3 To prevent the tea from seeping through the grain of the wood onto areas where you do not want it, incise carefully with a sharp craft knife along the lines of the design, to a depth of at least ¹⁄₁₆ in/2 mm.

4 Paint the tea solution inside the cut marks with a fine brush (inset). Do not paint right to the edge of your design, but allow the liquid to soak up to it. Place the object in a container with ammonia sulfate overnight (see p. 63). Where the tea solution was applied, the wood will darken and the design will stand out.

The Basic Technique: Bleaching

You can lighten dark and colored woods using speciality wood bleaches (household bleach will not work). A strong, effective bleach comes in two parts – or three parts including a neutralizer – and there are many proprietary brands. Wear protective gloves and a face mask when using wood bleach.

1 Apply Part A of the two-part bleach with a special vegetable-fiber bristle brush, which the bleach will not destroy. Leave for 5–10 minutes, or as directed on the instructions.

2 Apply Part B of the two-part bleach. The bleached surface will almost immediately begin to bubble (inset).

3 When the surface has dried, after a few hours, you will see how light the wood has become. To make it even lighter, repeat Step 2.

4 When the color is light enough, wash over the wood using the neutralizer suggested by the manufacturer. Allow to dry.

5 Wash the whole area with water to remove any traces of the neutralizer. Be careful not to over-saturate the wood.

6 The wood now appears lighter all over. Here, the oak has changed from a medium brown to a warm, pale yellow. If Part B was reapplied, the wood would be even whiter. You can now either use the bleached wood as it is, or you can stain it in some way.

Bleaching a Pattern

You can make simple patterns or designs in wood, such as on a tabletop or sections of furniture, using the two-part bleach. The bleach has a tendency to spread, working its way along the grain of the wood. To prevent this, use a craft knife to lightly incise the outline of the pattern into the wood.

1 Draw a simple pattern in pencil directly onto the wood. If the design is too intricate, especially on hardwood, it will be difficult to cut.

2 Using a sharp craft knife, incise the wood along your pattern to a depth of at least 1/16 in/2mm, to prevent the bleach from seeping along the grain.

3 Using an old brush, since the bleach will whiten the hairs, apply Part A of the bleach (see p. 65). Allow to dry for 5–10 minutes, or as instructed.

4 Apply Part B of the bleach, painting it in the same direction as the grain. Do not paint right to the edge of your design, but allow the liquid to soak up to it. When the surface has dried follow Steps 3–6 of The Basic Technique: Bleaching (see p. 65).

5 Here, the result is a precise, geometric pattern but you can easily create a more flowing design by applying both parts of the two-part bleach in dots.

Incised and Bleached Frame

RIGHT This oak frame was incised with a craft knife, making various geometric shapes. Parts of the frame were then bleached using the two-part bleach, to a near-white color, to create a sharp contrast with the dark, unbleached wood.

COLOR COMBINATIONS

Fumed/natural/bleached old pine

Fumed/natural/bleached new pine

Fumed/natural/bleached walnut

Fumed/natural/bleached mahogany

Bleached Tray

LEFT This walnut tray was painted with masking fluid in the shape of a tree and then bleached. When the masking fluid was removed, the tree motif remained unbleached. The whole tray was then covered with an oil-base varnish.

Bleached Table

RIGHT First the varnish was removed from alternate slats of this table. These were then bleached to a light, slightly pink-honey color, to create a striped effect.

Penwork

Penwork Box

This wooden box has penwork decoration, using both The Basic Technique *(see p. 69) and the* Dark Background *technique (see p. 70). The curved top, made of soft plywood, was sealed with four coats of sanding sealer to prevent the ink from running into the grain.*

T HIS TRADITIONAL TECHNIQUE is a method of allowing finely grained woods to contrast with an opaque layer of decoration in ink. India ink which is black and sepia – a warm, brown ink – are the most commonly used. Although the work looks meticulous and time-consuming, it is actually done quite quickly, once you have done the tracing. It is simply a matter of drawing around the design and filling in the spaces with ink, using mapping pens, calligraphy pens, or fine artist's brushes, all of which are available from art supply stores. You can use waterproof drawing ink or ordinary writing ink, which is more transparent and is not waterproof. Penwork is suited to pale, rather yellowish woods, since they contrast well with the darker ink. It is important to first seal the wood (see p. 12).

TOOLS & MATERIALS

India ink

Tracing paper and traced design

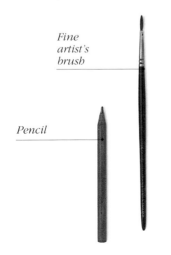

Mapping pen

Calligraphy pen

Fine artist's brush

Pencil

The Basic Technique

1 Trace a design. It is best to use simple repeated patterns which you can photocopy and, if necessary, enlarge to suit your project.

2 Having sealed the wood (see p. 12), transfer the design onto the surface using pigment and pencil (see p. 29).

3 Dip the nib of a mapping pen into the ink. On spare paper, remove any excess ink so that drips do not occur. First draw around the shapes, then fill in the centers.

4 Draw lines to separate different parts of the design. Practice first – raise the ruler slightly, load the nib with ink, then draw a line straight up until the ink runs out. Reload and start again, slightly overlapping the line where you finished.

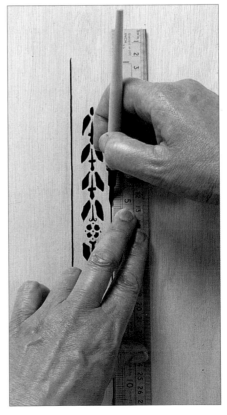

Dark Backgrounds

Trace and transfer a design (see p. 29) onto your sealed wood surface (see p. 12). Draw around the outline using a mapping pen. Instead of filling in the design, you fill in the background using a fine artist's brush. Apply a second coat of ink for a more solid background. Do not overload the brush with ink.

Using Diluted Ink

By using diluted ink (start with a ratio of 1 part ink to 1 part water), you can achieve a softer effect. Fill in the outline of your design with both diluted and undiluted ink to create shadows and depth.

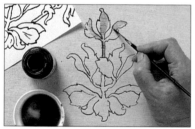

1 Dilute the ink, testing it on spare paper or wood and adjusting the strength if necessary. Using a fine artist's brush, apply the diluted ink to areas of the design, such as the central areas of the leaves and flowers, as here.

2 Add lines in undiluted ink, using a mapping pen to give definition to the design. Here, lines were applied to make leaf veins and add shadows.

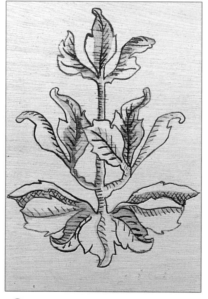

3 The finished effect includes cross-hatching, where you draw ink lines in opposite directions to emphasize dark areas.

PENSTROKES

Penwork was traditionally done with a fine mapping pen, but you can also use a calligraphy pen. Here, an angled, square-ended nib is used to create a wide variety of patterns, ranging from small diamond shapes to angular and wavy lines.

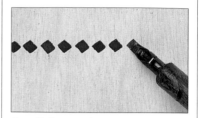

Small diamonds

The upward stroke is a thin line, the downward stroke is thick

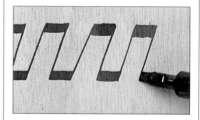

The downward stroke is a thin line, the horizontal stroke is thick

A looping line widens and narrows

Marquetry-style Corner Cupboard

RIGHT AND BELOW This pine corner cupboard has a design based on an antique chair decorated with marquetry work. The central brown stripe occurs naturally in the wood's grain. The penwork was done in India ink.

COLOR COMBINATIONS

Blue ink on poplar

India ink on poplar

Sepia Frame

LEFT The leaves and designs on this plain, modern pine frame were hand drawn using sepia-colored drawing ink. It was then coated with oil-base varnish.

Green ink on beech

1930s'-style Bowl

RIGHT The penwork on this small bowl made of wood from the rubber tree was done in green writing ink and brown drawing ink. The bowl was varnished using oil-base varnish to protect it and make it washable.

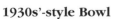

India and red ink on beech

Wax and Varnish
on Wood

Tools and Materials

WAXING FURNITURE IS POSSIBLY the oldest treatment for wood. It both protects the surface and treats it with oils to prevent the wood from drying out. The waxes enhance and help to bring out the natural grain of the wood. You can buy the white wax used for *Liming* (see p. 77) ready-made from art supply or hardware stores, or you can easily and inexpensively make it yourself by adding white pigment to clear wax. A clear or neutral wax can also be colored with other pigments to give an unusual finish, such as a bright blue.

Varnishes, as well as protecting wood, can be used to achieve a decorative finish. Add pigments to the varnish to change its basic color, or use precolored varnish, available from hardware stores. We use both water- and oil-base varnishes here, but if you are working on old furniture where previous treatments are not known, use oil-base varnish since water-base varnish may react and darken the surface where oil products were once used.

Fine steelwool

Waxes

RIGHT AND ABOVE These are non silicone-based speciality furniture waxes which are applied to the surface using fine steelwool. These waxes are readily available from hardware stores in both clear and colored forms. Precolored waxes are usually available in wood tones, but for brighter and more individual shades you can color waxes using pigments.

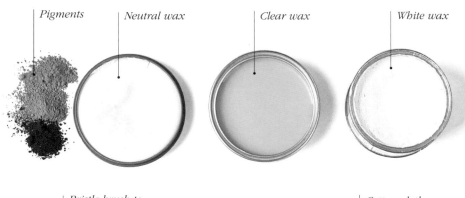

Pigments   *Neutral wax*   *Clear wax*   *White wax*

Finishing Touches

RIGHT The charm of a wax effect is that it can be buffed to a soft sheen for an extra finishing touch. You can buy bristle brushes for buffing or use a soft cotton cloth.

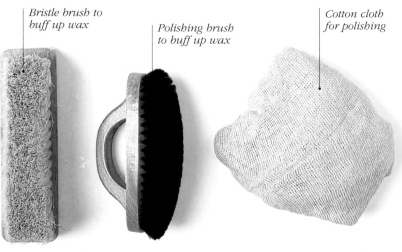

Bristle brush to buff up wax   *Polishing brush to buff up wax*   *Cotton cloth for polishing*

Water-base varnish and flat-ended, bristle varnish brush

Water-base Varnishes

LEFT Water-base varnish, also known as acrylic varnish, is often white or off-white in color. It dries completely clear and is available in flat, middle-sheen, and gloss finishes. Water-base varnish can easily be colored by adding pigment, or bought precolored. The advantage of water-base varnish is the ease of washing the brushes afterwards. Use flat-ended bristle varnish brushes to apply water-base varnish.

Flat-ended, bristle varnish brush

Brown pigment

Green pigment

Blue pigment

Oil-base Varnishes

BELOW Oil-base varnish, sometimes called polyurethane varnish, is clear but dries with a slight yellowish tinge. It can be bought in flat, middle-sheen, or gloss finishes. You can color oil-base varnishes using pigments or buy them precolored. After using oil-base varnish, wash your brush in mineral spirits/turpentine.

Mineral spirits/ turpentine

Precolored oil-base varnish

Oil-base varnish

Flat-ended, soft-haired varnish brushes

Shellac

BELOW Shellac is available in varying depths of color, from deep brown (Garnet Polish) and red-brown (Button Polish) to amber (French Polish). It dries very quickly and gives a high gloss finish. You can add bronze powders to shellac to give a look resembling Chinese lacquer. After using shellac, wash your brushes in denatured alcohol/methylated spirits.

Denatured alcohol/ methylated spirits

Garnet Polish shellac

Button Polish shellac

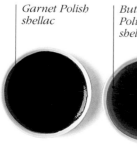

French Polish shellac and flat-ended, soft-haired varnish brush for applying shellac

Using Colored Waxes

Waxed Bed Headboard
This dark, old oak bed headboard was stripped of varnish and waxed all over with white wax to give it a clean, limed, country appearance.

TREATING WOOD WITH WAX is longlasting and gives a beautiful soft sheen. White wax, or clear or neutral wax colored with pigments, is worked into the grain of the wood and buffed with a soft cloth. You can buy white wax as a proprietary product or you can make it at home simply by taking a clear wax and adding white pigment until you get the right tone. You can also make as many colored waxes as there are pigments. The final color you achieve is affected strongly by the color of the wood underneath. You can also apply a pattern, using a stencil and colored waxes. Using wax to bring out the grain of the wood works best on woods with a pronounced grain, such as oak, ash, chestnut, elm, pitch pine, and teak.

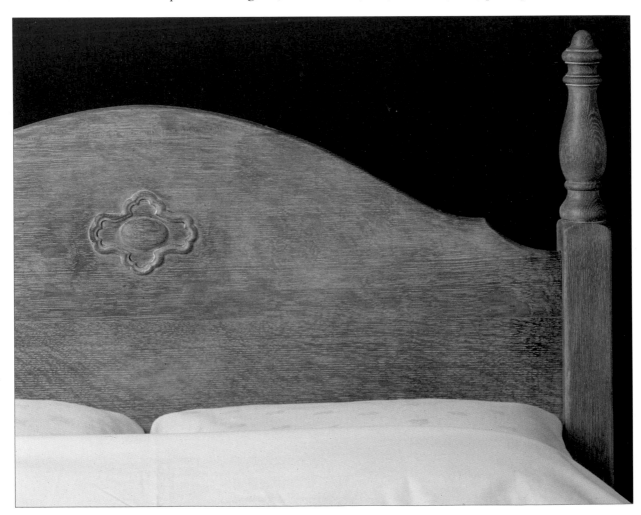

TOOLS & MATERIALS

Phosphor bronze
wire brush

Fine
steelwool

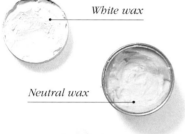

White wax

Neutral wax

Cotton cloth

Pigment,
neutral wax,
and palette
knife for mixing

Stencil and
stencil brush

The Basic Technique: Liming

1 It is useful, although not essential, to open up the grain of the wood by rubbing it hard with a phosphor bronze wire brush along the grain, so that the wax will sit in it well.

2 Using fine steelwool, apply white wax generously, first across the grain and then along it. Leave for a few minutes for the solvents to evaporate, but do not allow it to dry.

3 With a fresh piece of steelwool, rub all over the wood in both directions to remove excess wax.

4 To remove more wax so that the white remains only in the recessed grain, rub over the surface with a clear wax on fine steelwool.

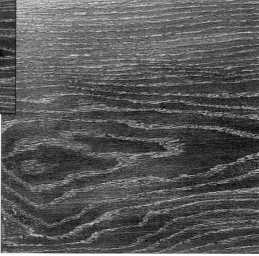

5 Use more steelwool to remove the final traces of wax and buff the surface to a soft sheen with a clean cotton cloth (inset). The white wax brings out the grain in the wood.

Coloring Wax

1 *Mix pigment and neutral or clear wax (here, 2 parts wax to 1 part pigment) with a palette knife.*

2 *Using fine steelwool, apply the wax generously to the wood, working it into the surface in all directions.*

3 *Remove the excess wax with a fresh piece of steelwool. You can work on the wood again the next day to build up a deeper, richer color.*

Applying Wax to a Stencil

By using pigments to color waxes, you can paint a stencil design directly onto wood. The design will have a delicate sheen, but it will not withstand wear and tear unless you protect it with a coat of shellac (see p. 20).

1 *Mix the neutral or clear wax and pigments, using a stencil brush. Position a simple stencil using masking tape.*

2 *Remove any excess wax from the brush. Rub onto the wood from the sides of the stencil to avoid a buildup along the edges.*

3 *Remove the stencil to see if the colors work well and show up successfully against the background. Redo any areas that are not strong enough.*

4 *The finished design is a mixture of colors, with the colors on the leaves and acorns blending together. Here, the oak motif was stenciled against a walnut wood background.*

COLOR COMBINATIONS

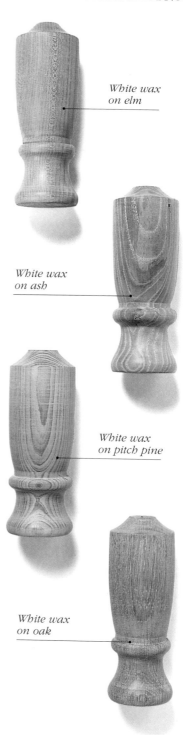

White wax on elm

White wax on ash

White wax on pitch pine

White wax on oak

Limed Cabinet Door
BELOW *A carved oak door from a 1930s' sideboard was stripped and waxed with white wax to create this limed effect.*

Red-waxed Lampbase
ABOVE *This ash lampbase was waxed with a mixture of wax and red pigment (2 parts wax to 1 part pigment).*

Black-and-white-waxed Chest of Drawers
ABOVE *Black-pigmented wax (2 parts wax to 1 part pigment) was used on the top and framework of this oak chest of drawers. A proprietary white wax was applied to the drawers.*

Using Colored Varnishes

Varnished Chest of Drawers

This new pine chest of drawers is varnished using dark brown and three shades of red varnish in a loose design. The final result looks quite modern.

THE ADVANTAGE OF USING VARNISH to achieve a decorative finish is that you can decorate and protect a piece of furniture at the same time. Traditional varnishes have an oil base or are based on denatured alcohol/methylated spirits. They impart a warm yellow hue. Modern varnishes have a water base. They dry quickly and brushes are easily cleaned with water. The type that you choose – oil- or water-base, flat, middle-sheen, or glossy – is a matter of personal preference. Any varnishes can be colored with pigments, but precolored varnishes are also available.

TOOLS & MATERIALS

Oil-base varnish

Red pigment

Yellow pigment

Round-ended, hard-bristled brush

Flat-ended, bristle brush for use with water-base varnish

Flat-ended, soft-haired brush for use with oil-base varnish

Fine artist's brush

Water-base varnish

Flat-ended, soft-haired brush

Shellac

Bronze powder

The Basic Technique

You can use pigment to color oil- or water-base varnishes. When applied, the varnish should look colored but transparent, so that the wood shows through. Bear in mind that if the piece you are varnishing is already colored, this base color may affect the final color.

1 In a bowl, press out any lumps in your pigment with any hard-bristled brush (inset). Add a little varnish, stirring continuously (about 3 level teaspoons of pigment to 1 pint/600ml of varnish will make a transparent color). Mix up enough varnish to cover your whole surface at one time, using the instructions on the varnish to aid in calculating this. Test for transparency on some spare wood.

2 Having sealed your surface (see p. 12), apply the varnish using a flat-ended varnish brush, spreading it out thinly over the surface.

3 Feather out the varnish, using the tip of the brush at right angles to the surface. Avoid drips, especially on vertical planes. Allow to dry for 30 minutes to 1 hour.

4 You can apply a second or third color in the same way to create a pattern. Bear in mind that where there are three layers of color the varnish is almost opaque.

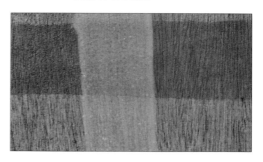

Dripping Varnish

In this technique, splashes of clear, oil- or water-base varnish are dropped onto a still-wet layer of colored varnish, then blotted off using a brush. The splashes of varnish come off easily, revealing the wood underneath. Here, pigment colors the varnish, but you can use precolored varnish.

1 Apply a generous coat of clear varnish – here, oil-base – spreading it with the varnish brush. Do not allow it to become so thin that it dries.

2 Dip your brush into the pigment and spread out the color on the still-wet varnish. Some areas will look darker than others.

3 Dip the brush into a second pigment and brush it on in patches over the first color. The colors should blend in a cloudy, random way.

4 Dip a round-ended, bristle brush into clear oil-base varnish and drip it onto the still-wet varnished surface. Allow to settle for a few minutes.

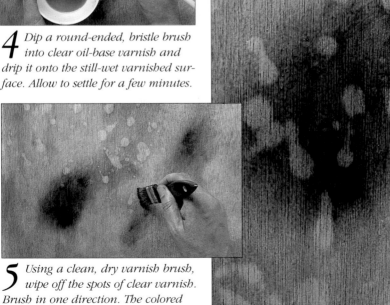

5 Using a clean, dry varnish brush, wipe off the spots of clear varnish. Brush in one direction. The colored varnish is removed by the clear varnish, revealing the wood base.

Making a Design in Varnish

This technique is similar to that of *Dripping Varnish* (see p. 82). Onto a still wet coat of colored, oil- or water-base varnish you apply a design in clear oil- or water-base varnish. When you blot the design with a clean brush both layers of varnish are easily removed, revealing the base wood.

1 *Mix your varnish – here, water-base varnish, which looks white before use – with a little pigment. Test for translucency on some spare wood or a hidden surface.*

2 *Apply the colored varnish using a varnish brush, spreading it thinly over the surface and making sure it does not dry out.*

3 *With a fine artist's brush, draw your design in clear, water-base varnish. Keep the design simple so that it is quick to apply and the clear varnish does not have time to dry out.*

4 *Using a clean, dry varnish brush, wipe off the still-wet clear varnish in the patterned area (inset). The wet varnish will remove the undercoat of colored varnish, leaving a design through which the wood shows clearly.*

Metallic Varnish

This technique mixes shellac and bronze powder to give a look resembling Chinese lacquer. It is also known as Vernis Martin, named after the Martin brothers who first developed the technique in Paris in about 1730.

1 *Add some gold-colored bronze powder to shellac (see p. 75) and mix well with any small brush. Test for translucency on some spare wood or a hidden surface.*

2 *Paint the shellac onto the wooden surface, using a flat-ended, soft-haired varnish brush. Work quickly and do not over-brush one area.*

3 *The finished result will look different, depending on the light and the angle from which you view it. From some angles it will look gold; from some, glittering with specks of gold and the wood apparent underneath; from others, no gold at all will be visible.*

PITFALLS
With all colored-varnish work, the main danger is applying too much color or bronze powder so that you cannot see the wood surface below. Test the varnish for transparency on spare wood before you begin.

Patterned Spindle

LEFT AND BELOW This pine staircase spindle was varnished with green then yellow oil-base varnish. It was then dabbed all over several times with a crumpled up dry rag to remove some of the varnish, revealing the wooden base.

Lined Wastebasket

ABOVE A brown water-base varnish was painted all over this wastebasket. Clear water-base varnish was then dribbled down the sides to create a series of lines, and blotted off with a brush. Brown water-base varnish was painted at the base.

Colored Plate Rack

ABOVE *A new pine plate rack was painted using several different colored varnishes. Clear oil-base varnish was applied in patterns around the cabinet and removed to reveal the wood base.*

Patterned Panel

BELOW *Colored water-base varnishes were removed in places with a clear varnish to create patterns.*

COLOR COMBINATIONS

Deep terra-cotta, blues, green, and purple on oak

Pastel pink, blue, green, and browns on pale sycamore

Bright greens, blues, and terra-cotta on pitch pine

White, yellow, blues, and terra-cotta on mahogany

Varnished Frame

ABOVE *A small pine frame was varnished using blue pigment brushed into oil-base varnish. Spots of clear oil-base varnish were dropped on, then wiped off to reveal the base. An oil-base varnish colored with red-brown pigment was then applied all over.*

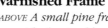

Combining Techniques

S O FAR ALL THE PROJECTS in this book use just one technique. Often, however, you can combine several techniques on one piece of furniture. In this section two or more techniques are shown working together. You can, for instance, stain woods – using both modern and homemade stains – before adding a painted decoration, such as hand painting, stenciling, or metal leaf. Stains are very useful as the basecoat for a piece of furniture since stains can enhance the wood, making an effective background for further embellishment. Fuming and bleaching act in the same way. You could also choose to use colored varnishes and waxes as a finish in combination with stains and paints. The possibilities for combining different techniques on one item are as limitless as your imagination.

Penwork and Embellished Leaf Dish

BELOW Green ink was used to make the leaflike veins on this shaped cedar dish. The edge of the dish was defined using loose Dutch metal leaf. The top of the dish was coated with an oil-base varnish, leaving the underneath unsealed so that the appealing smell of the wood is still apparent.

Penwork (see pp. 68–71)

Painting and Embellishing Wood (see pp. 28–33)

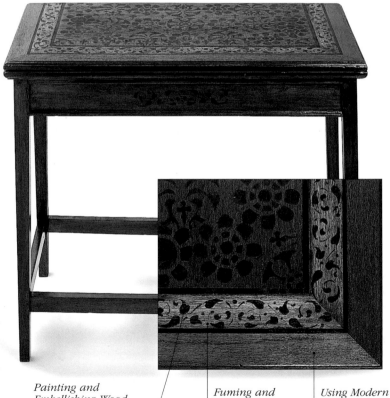

Bleached, Stained, and Stenciled Table

RIGHT The border on this tabletop was bleached a pale cream color. Then the entire table was washed with a green water-base stain. The tabletop was then stenciled, using green water-base paint and varnished for protection.

Painting and Embellishing Wood (see pp. 28–33)

Fuming and Bleaching (see pp. 62–67)

Using Modern Stains (see pp. 56–61)

Embellished, Stained, and Waxed Mirror

RIGHT AND BELOW Loose Dutch metal leaf was used to enhance the carved wooden panel and edgings of this mirror. The rest of the wood was rubbed with a green-blue wax.

Painting and Distressing (see pp. 44–47)

Revealing Wood Under Paint (see pp. 40–43)

Painting and Embellishing Wood (see pp. 28–33)

Using Colored Waxes (see pp. 76–79)

Revealed and Distressed Chair

RIGHT AND ABOVE The olive-green paint on this chair was stripped away in random patches using paint stripper. Clear wax was applied to the legs and back of the chair. Lines of red water-base paint were added, then rubbed with fine steelwool to create the aged look.

Painting and Distressing (see pp. 44–47)

Fumed, Stenciled, and Distressed Frame

RIGHT This new oak frame was fumed to give it a mellow, older-looking brown color. Clear wax was applied in places and a latticework design was stenciled on using a dark red water-base paint. Finally, the waxed areas were rubbed with steelwool to give a distressed effect.

Fuming and Bleaching (see pp. 62–67)

Painting and Embellishing Wood (see pp. 28–33)

Stained and Distressed Table

RIGHT Clear wax was rubbed onto parts of the side and top of this table. A light brown water-base stain was applied all over and a darker brown stain rubbed into the carving. Red and green water-base stains were stenciled on the tabletop. Coarse steel-wool was used to wipe back the colors both on the top and sides of the table so that the natural wood showed through in places. The table was finished with a very dark wax to give it a unified effect.

Painting and Distressing (see pp. 44–47)

Using Modern Stains (see pp. 56–61)

Waxed, Stained, and Hand-painted Lampbase

RIGHT This small oak lampbase was colored by rubbing a blue wax deep into the grain. A brown oil-base stain was then used to paint leaf shapes, lines, and spots. These were later highlighted with a green water-base paint.

Painting and Embellishing Wood (see pp. 28–33)

Using Modern Stains (see pp. 56–61)

Using Colored Waxes (see pp. 76–79)

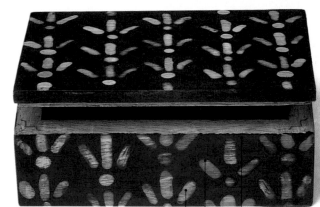

Stained and Revealed Box

ABOVE A yellow homemade stain covers this box. Flower shapes were painted in masking fluid, using regular spacing. A black oil-base stain was painted on top and the masking fluid removed to reveal the stained wood beneath.

Using Modern Stains (see pp. 56–61)

Using Homemade Stains (see pp. 52–55)

Revealing Wood Under Paint (see pp. 40–43)

Stained and Penworked Bowl

RIGHT Patches of light and medium brown were made on this bowl by painting on spots using a homemade stain made with various ratios of ferrous sulfate to water. India ink was then painted on top to create the tortoiseshell or animal-skin look.

Penwork (see pp. 68–71)

Using Homemade Stains (see pp. 52–55)

Bleached and Stained Tray

LEFT A tree design was painted on this small walnut tray using masking fluid. The tray was then bleached and the masking fluid removed to reveal the original wood color. A water-base stain was applied to the leaves and grass, giving color and definition.

Fuming and Bleaching (see pp. 62–67)

Painting and Embellishing Wood (see pp. 28–33)

Using Colored Varnishes (see pp. 80–85)

Using Modern Stains (see pp. 56–61)

Using Modern Stains (see pp. 56–61)

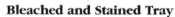

Hand-painted, Varnished, and Stained Pencil Box

RIGHT To give this pale-colored pencil box some character, small birds were painted on the lid and front using water-base paint. They were then covered with an oil-base varnish colored with a little brown pigment. The top edge was stained with a black oil-base stain.

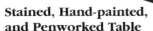

Stained, Hand-painted, and Penworked Table

RIGHT This new pine tabletop was colored with blue pigment stain. A design of arches and leaves was added in blue and sepia drawing ink with washes of diluted ink in places. Blue water-base paint was applied to the base and rim of the table and the table was varnished for protection.

Penwork (see pp. 68–71)

Using Homemade Stains (see pp. 52–55)

Painting and Embellishing Wood (see pp. 28–33)

Stained and Distressed Box

LEFT The top of this birch box was painted with a white water-base stain. The grain of the wood suggested a landscape so green, brown, and blue water-base stains were used to depict trees and a foreground. The molded sides of the box were coated with clear wax and painted with an oil-base stain, then distressed with steelwool to reveal the old brown stain underneath.

Using Modern Stains (see pp. 56–61)

Painting and Distressing (see pp. 44–47)

Using Colored Varnishes (see pp. 80–85)

Painting and Embellishing Wood (see pp. 28–33)

Stenciled and Varnished Box

LEFT AND ABOVE This pine box was first stenciled with a simple design of lines in a very pale brown-gray water-base paint. An oil-base varnish colored with black pigment was then applied and clear varnish was randomly dropped on top, making circular spots.

Woodgrained and Stained Cabinet

RIGHT AND BELOW The technique of bird's eye maple woodgraining was used on the main part of this pine cabinet, which was stained with a blue water-base stain on the inside. An oil-base stain was used on the molding, after incising the wood to prevent the stain from spreading.

Using Modern Stains (see pp. 56–61)

Woodgraining (see pp. 34–39)

Revealed and Penworked Chair

BELOW Paint stripper was used to paint designs on the back and legs of this chair, removing the varnish and revealing the lighter wood beneath. This was then stained with a water-base yellow stain and highlighted with red ink.

Penwork (see pp. 68–71)

Using Modern Stains (see pp. 56–61)

Revealing Wood Under Paint (see pp. 40–43)

Stained and Revealed Bowl

BELOW The outside of this balsa-wood bowl was stained using Van Dyck crystals and painted with pale blue water-base paint. A modern abstract pattern was applied in paint stripper on the sides, revealing the stained wood underneath.

Revealing Wood Under Paint (see pp. 40–43)

Using Homemade Stains (see pp. 52–55)

Index

How to Find Supplies

The tools and materials you need for the techniques demonstrated in this book are generally available from hardware stores or speciality paint stores. To find a store near you, try looking in your local telephone directory under paint, craft supplies, decorative materials, or decorator's supplies. If you are on the Internet, you can look there under the same categories, or you can try speciality magazines on crafts and interior decoration, where many of the stores and suppliers place advertisements. If there are no stores in your neighborhood, don't despair as many of them have mail order facilities and you can send for a catalogue.

You can also visit Annie Sloan's Internet site – *www.anniesloan.co.uk* – for more information.

Acknowledgments

The same terrific team of people have been responsible for this book and for the other books in the same series. In the studio were the designer Steve Wooster, the photographer Geoff Dann and his assistant Gavin Durrant, and Liz Penny, provider of refreshments and props. In the office thanks as usual to Colin Ziegler, Claire Waite, and Mandy Greenfield for their care and consideration.

Back at home and in the paint studio my husband David Manuel and my children Henry, Felix, and Hugo have all been tremendously supportive and helpful of an, at times, very cantankerous author. Many thanks also to Wendy Rawlins and Emma Brooklyn for good humored help in trying to keep me tidy.

The Shaker boxes, trays, and pails were supplied by A. B. Woodworking (Unit J, Pentre Wern, Gobowen, Oswestry, SY10 7JZ Tel: 01691 670425). Thanks to Jane Warwick for help providing furniture to work on and to David Wessex (Wessex Timber, Longney, Gloucester, GL2 3SJ Tel: 01452 740610) who gave expert help and guidance on the woods.

Thanks also to Bret Wiles of Relics of Witney for providing invaluable help with some basic wood techniques and checking the manuscript and to Chris Walker and Ray Russell also of Relics.